DESTINY MOMENTS

DESTINY MOMENTS
JEFF CRUME

Jeff Crume Ministries Publishing

DEDICATION

To my wife, Jodi, and our four children:
Kami, Talia, Luke & Braeden–
my greatest *destiny moments*.

Contents

Introduction xi

1 Seven Days In Utopia 14

2 Underground 17

3 Move It or Go With It 19

4 The Right Formula 21

5 Put Feet To Your Faith 23

6 The Miracle of Giving 25

7 Are You My Mother? 28

8 No One Loves A Self-righteous Savior 30

9 My Quirk & My Value 34

10 Deep In It 37

11 Don't Let Your Next
Opportunity Find You In Rollers 41

12 Maturity & Immaturity 45

13 Monsters In The Closet 47

14 What Are You Waiting On? 51

15 Where Does God
Find His Next American Idol? 54

16 Let Zealous Indignation Arise! 57

17 Don't Settle For Sour 59

18 Don't Be Too Quick
To Build A Tabernacle 61

19 Perfection 64

20 Thrive, Don't Strive 69

21 The Missing Link 71

About the Author 74

My Moments (Record your destiny moments) 74

ACKNOWLEDGEMENTS

My Wife,
Jodi—
Thank you for standing by my side
every moment of my journey, and for believing
in me when I didn't believe in myself.

My Children,
Kami, Talia, Luke & Braeden—
Thank you for being my reasons for living.

My Friends,
Lois & Gerson—
Thank you for sticking closer than a brother.

My Lord,
Jesus—
Thank you dying for me. And for
calling me to preach.

My Mom—
Thank you for dragging me to Church
every time the doors were open.

My Editor
Erika—
Thank you for dotting my i's
and crossing my t's.

Introduction

Destiny doesn't happen by chance; it happens in the fullness of, and at the appointed time.

Some things in life you ask for and simply receive. Other things you have to seek out and find, or discover. Things you receive are simple to explain and easy to describe—*it looks like, tastes like, feels like*—but things you discover are a bit more complicated.

Discoveries consist of sudden bursts, feelings, revelations, epiphanies, ideas, or moments, all rolled into a jolt that reverberates through your soul. When moments like this hit you, you try your hardest to figure out what just happened, but you can't put your finger on it; you just know something has happened. It's like a subtle bomb goes off inside, revealing to you that a life-altering moment, a destiny moment, has just occurred.

I'm convinced that these moments are encounters with our very own destiny. Deep within the human soul and spirit, waiting to be discovered, waiting to be fulfilled is destiny—one's divine purpose, life mission, and assignment. Destiny moments happen when *You* collide with the *You* that you were created to be.

Destiny doesn't happen by chance; it happens in the fullness of, and at the appointed time. Destiny is the deliberate fulfillment of purpose at the divinely appointed time. You don't sneak up on Destiny. You don't take Destiny by surprise.

Do You Have The Time?

If you asked the average person, "Do you have the time?" almost 100% of them would pull out their iPhone and say, "Sure, the time is…" But a person of destiny doesn't look to the outside to tell time, but to the inside.

A person of destiny has an internal clock deep within their soul that has been recording every second and every minute, every pain and every sorrow, and every victory and every defeat of their journey and knows, without looking, "it's my time now!"

On the following pages are scribed some of my own *destiny moments*—life-altering moments that I've encountered over the past thirty years of pursuing my destiny. These moments have come, as yours will, at a great price of heartache and pain, joy and sorrow, and fear and faith. They have led me to a deep understanding and absolute certainty of *Whose* I am, of *Who* I am, and *What* I am on this earth to do.

To My Reader

It is my earnest prayer that reading this book is one of your own destiny moments. That somehow, someway the words penned on these pages will ignite in you a chain reaction of moments—*destiny moments*—that will forever alter your life and set you on course for destiny.

Guided prayers follow many of the destiny moments I've written. These prayers are not to be used as some religious rule or ritual, but simply to "prime your pump" and help draw out of you what's taken me a lifetime to discover on my own.

A Special Request

I only ask one thing in return; that as you finish this book you make a promise to yourself to begin recording your own destiny moments, and then leave those moments for others who will follow in your footsteps to discover.

The greatest treasures you could leave behind are the moments you've encountered while you are on this earth. What takes one a lifetime to learn, another can read in a moment and instantly be changed. Also, would you please send me an e-mail, a letter, or a card, and let me know how this book has impacted your life.

Thank you for giving me the privilege and honor of speaking into your life through this book. May you find and fulfill you divine destiny.

—Jeff Crume

1 SEVEN DAYS IN UTOPIA

I live to reflect, not to attract. I live to reveal, not to retain. I point the way; I am not the way. If my life helps someone else see the way, I am complete.

My family and I watched a movie called Seven Days in Utopia. I thought I was in for a good golf movie with a happy ending. What I got was a message of life, of faith, and of destiny that changed me forever.

The movie is actually one long evangelistic outreach message with an *altar call* at the end. The altar call is in the form of instructions at the end of the movie to visit a website to see the ending of the movie. On the website, for seven minutes or so, the producers recap and reinforce their message of Utopia, and set the hook in you for the sequel. The underlying message speaks loud and clear. *"My destiny is not about me."*

My Destiny Is Not About Me

I've heard that all my life. I've preached it from the pulpit countless times. Yet watching the movie, I experienced the meaning. True success is on the other side of the finish line. There is an awareness of living for yourself and your world.

I know firsthand the feeling of getting up every day pursuing destiny. I work hard doing things that develop me as a person, make life better for my family, and advance my dream. But, living beyond the finish is even higher.

Living beyond the finish line is not even about people, necessarily, it's just an awareness of life from a higher perspective. Your view of things is now from 30,000 feet rather than what is directly in front of you.

Living Beyond The Finish Line

The revelation of living beyond the finish line is what has been missing in my life. Now, if you would have asked me I would have never been able to tell you it was missing, because I didn't even know this perspective existed. I didn't know what life looked like from *up here.*

There have been times in my life when I finally had *arrived*–I thought. I had made it to what God had created me for. But living to arrive is so shallow. I didn't know it then, but I see it now. *Living to arrive is living on this side of the finish line*, or for the finish line at best. It's living to say you lived, doing for the sake of doing, just so you can say you did it and have the trophy to show for it.

If trophies and accolades, money or fame brought fulfillment, why are so many people living miserable lives? Or worse yet, dying young with a wall, drawer, or a house full of trophies or money?

Seven Days in Utopia opened my eyes to living for more than just myself, more than just my dream, even more than just my family or people. It opened my eyes to a Higher Calling.

A Higher Calling

I'm not talking about a one-time religious experience. I'm talking about living in oneness with The One who created me. It's about living with the understanding that everyday my footsteps are in line with the Divine plan for my life. It's not that I'm doing what I've always dreamed of, it's the fact I'm doing what I was created to do. Living with the perspective of "my dream" is still living on this side of the finish line.

We were created for fellowship, for oneness with the Creator. We were never created to just work, do, be, go, or accomplish. If we were created to be known for what we did, we should create a video player epithet and just replay all the awards and trophies we received and things we accomplished. That's why they make an epithet so small, because there is not room for a list of things, just a few words.

It's not about getting a trophy. I am a trophy of the Greatest One that ever lived.

The One who is, who was, and who is to come. I am a clay vessel in the hands of the Master Potter. I reflect Him and His desire for my design. My desires for my design no longer matter. I live for Him, not for me.

I live to reflect, not to attract. I live to reveal, not to retain. I point the way; I am not the way. If my life helps someone else see the way, I am complete.

2 Underground

Don't mistake underground with underdeveloped,
unused, ineffective, insignificant, or unimportant
Visibility is not an indication of ability.

*T*he greatest undertakings are prepared underground. We only glance at average size trees, but we stand in awe of those that tower above all the rest. The taller the tree, the longer it remains underground.

A tree that lives a long time above ground has lived even longer underground. *A great tree has been great long before it is ever noticed.* The longer it remains underground, the longer it lives above ground.

Everyone loves to be seen. Yet it is wisdom to desire to be unseen until it's your time. There's a time I long to be seen, there's a time I endure being seen, and then there's a time I wish I was never seen. There's a time one desires to be known, there's a time one endures being known, and there's a time one wishes they were never known.

Until now, you have been functioning *underground*. You have been in hiding, a secret operation beneath the surface and out of view. But the ground has broken open. The earth has made a way for you. You are bursting forth. *The time for you to be seen is now!*

They will stop to say, "I've never seen that tree before. Where did it come from?" You are about to hear, "Where did you come from?" This is said most of those who remain underground the longest.

If you had been seen any sooner, you would have been a one-hit-wonder. If you had been given what you thought you wanted any earlier, you would have nothing to show for it.

What isn't seen develops; what is seen nourishes. The longer you remain unseen, the more you have to nourish.

Don't mistake underground with underdeveloped, unused, ineffective, insignificant, or unimportant. Visibility is not an indication of ability. People who remain underground are protected from the scrutiny of public opinion until they can withstand the pressures associated with notoriety.

Obscurity has now prepared you for the scrutiny of notoriety.

Guided Prayer:

Father, help me to be content with being known only by you, until it's time for me to be known by others.

3 MOVE IT OR GO WITH IT

*Overwhelming desire to fulfill your destiny can make
you vulnerable to unwarranted stress or anxiety.*

*T*here are times in your journey when you need to gather
every ounce of strength you have in order to MOVE
whatever is in your way. Stay up late, get up early, do whatever
you have to do to resist and remove that which is coming
against you.

However, there are other times when you really need to just
"go with the flow." Nothing is wrong, it's not an attack, God is
not trying to tell you something; you are simply having "one of
those days."

It's important for you to discern what season you are in so
that you know how to respond to the thing that is coming
against you. You can easily be taken off course, or hinder your
own progress, by giving too much concern to things that are of
no significance.

Be careful you don't allow yourself to make something out of
nothing just so you have something to complain, I mean, talk
about. Your destiny is the most important focus of life. Your
overwhelming desire to fulfill it can make you vulnerable to
unwarranted stress or anxiety.

Remember, "Be anxious for nothing"

Are you going where you are supposed to go, doing what you are supposed to do, but still running into difficulty? Take heart. It's not the devil, it's not God, and it's not even you. It's life!

Don't waste your energy trying to move it, *go with it*. Simply grin and bear it. *Remember, this too shall pass!*

4 The Right Formula

A formula begins with the creation in its finished form and works backward.

*E*veryone is always looking for the "right formula." What I have the formula for I have the potential benefit of.

If I know the right formula for a good marriage, I have the potential benefit of a good marriage. If I know the right formula for a successful business, I have the potential benefit of a successful business.

A formula is like a key that unlocks the mystery behind the way something is. If I discover the formula and apply it correctly, I receive the benefit of what the formula has to offer. But a formula is someone's discovery of something that already is. *A formula doesn't create; it defines what already is. A formula begins with the creation in its finished form and works backward.*

The Bible says in Genesis 1:27, "So God created man in his [own] image, in the image of God created he him; male and female..." The "finished image" of Man is the image of God. Hebrews 12:2 says, "Looking unto Jesus the *author and finisher of* [our] faith."

Jesus Christ is the finished image of our faith. In other words, faith doesn't create or make me into the image of Christ; faith reveals that I am already made in His likeness. Ephesians

2:5-6 declares, "Even when we were dead in sins, [He] hath quickened us together with Christ, (by grace ye are saved;) And hath raised us up together, and made us sit together in heavenly places in Christ Jesus:"

Many of us use God's Word and the principles of God to "make us" someone or somebody "better," when actually *the Bible is not a formula that makes you anybody; but reveals to you who you already are.* The more you know who you are, the more you will begin to act like it.

Starting today, look into the Scriptures with a new attitude. Attend your worship service this week with a different perspective. When you hear your minister or pastor talking about *the righteous* and *the redeemed*, when you read scriptures about *the blessed* and *the beloved*, just smile and say to yourself, "he (or she) is talking about *me!*"

5 Put Feet To Your Faith

*Faith is the unseen power that pushes one through
the pain and pressure required to attain the unseen.*

What good is it to say you have faith when you have nothing to show for it? If someone comes to you in need of food and you tell them to have faith, and send them away but never give them food, what good are you?

Faith is the power that moves mountains. Faith is the power that creates new life. Faith is the force of God Almighty in a human being that changes circumstances, transforms lives, and sets the captives free.

Many shout about faith, sing about faith, even brag about faith, but *if you don't have any works to back up your faith, your faith is nothing but hot air, even verging on hypocritical.*

Faith without works is dead—destitute of force or power, inactive, and inoperative. Saying that you have faith doesn't mean you have faith.

Work is the corresponding action to faith that produces results. Work is the human effort that, combined with the force of faith, produces lasting change. Faith fuels action.

Faith is the unseen power that pushes one through the pain and pressure required to attain the unseen. Faith declares, "On the other side of this effort is my reward and promise." Faith without action remains a fantasy. You cannot create lasting change with fantasy.

If I'm hungry, I don't need your faith. I need your food. If my car is out of gas, I don't need your faith. I need fuel. You see, real faith is in the action of giving of the food to the one who is hungry. Real faith is in the action of giving fuel to the one who has run out of gas. Real faith is in the corresponding action of who you say you are and what you say you can do.

If you say you can… then *show me*! If you say you are…then *show me*! Stop telling me and *show me*! And by the way, do the world a favor, if you can't back up what you say then stop saying anything at all!

Too many people have already been hurt by faith-talking, but not faith-walking, people.

The next time you are in a position to let your faith do the talking, may I suggest you *put feet to your faith* and let your faith do the walking instead? Fill someone's gas tank, buy someone's lunch, help clean up after everyone is gone.

Temporary change comes by what you say, but lasting change comes by what you do!

6 The Miracle of Giving

*When one gives away what they were going
to use for themselves to someone in need,
a supernatural principle takes place.*

$\mathcal{H}$ ave you ever wondered what you were created for? Have you ever wondered if you were really created to be someone important?

Do you know that you have a purpose? Yes, you! You have a purpose. Want to know what that purpose is? It is to give! That's right, *your purpose is to give.*

The greatest miracle of giving ever recorded is found in the Bible. John 3:16 says, "God so loved the world that He gave His only..." The greatest motivating factor of giving is also found in this text—*Love.*

The text says that God so *loved* that He *gave.* Love motivates the miracle of giving. Many people give to get, or give because of how it makes them feel or look. However, true giving is motivated by love.

Giving Your Only

The second principle of the miracle of giving is *giving your only.* When one gives away what they were going to use for themselves to someone else in need, a supernatural principle takes place. Know what it is? *Multiplication.*

Multiplication

Multiplication is the supernatural principle that "kicks in," or that is activated, when we give out of *love* and we give our *only*.

Take for instance another story in the Bible found in 1 Kings 17. The Prophet Elijah was told by God to go to a place called Zarephath. God also told Elijah that a widow would provide for him.

I find that odd. A widow is someone who can barely take care of herself most of the time. How in the world would a widow take care of herself and the Prophet too? *By giving!*

The story reads that when Elijah got to Zarephath, he saw a widow gathering sticks. He asked her to get him some water that he could drink. As she was going to fetch the water, Elijah asked the widow to bring him a morsel of bread too.

The widow said, "As the Lord thy God liveth, I have not a cake, but a handful of meal in a barrel, and a little oil in a cruse: and behold, I am gathering two sticks, that I may go in and dress it for me and my son, that we may eat it, and die."

Elijah told the woman, "Go and do as you have said, but make me therefore a little cake first, and bring it to me, and after make for thee and for thy son. For the Lord God of Israel says to you that the barrel of meal shall not waste, neither shall the cruse of oil fail, until the Lord sends rain upon the earth."

Now obviously there was a famine in the land and the famine was because there was no rain. Everyone was in need, because there was no meal being harvested and no trading going on.

This poor woman found herself with just enough meal and oil to make a cake for her and her son, which they were going to eat and die. Here comes the miracle working process. The Prophet said, "Give me some first and then go bake some for yourself."

I don't know about you friend, but if I only had enough for myself and my son it wouldn't make sense for me to give what I had away; especially to a total stranger.

But Elijah wasn't just a stranger; *he was a prophet of God.* In other words, *he was a representation of God's work.* And when the Widow gave the "first" of what she had to the work of God, God turned around and blessed what she "had left." The woman was so blessed that she had enough to go on for her and her son until the rain came, which caused the harvest of grain to come again and supply her needs.

If you've ever wondered what you were created for, **you were created to give**.

I challenge you, right now, even in times of hardship—GIVE! Find someone in need, and give what you had reserved for yourself. Watch and see if God will not open the windows of heaven and pour out a blessing on your home and all that is yours.

Guided Prayer:

Father, give me a giving heart. Transform me by the power of your love that I may love those in need, so much so, that I give what I have reserved for myself. And I thank you, Father, as I do give, all of my needs are met according to your riches and glory, amen.

7 ARE YOU MY MOTHER?

*Your dream is looking for you
just as hard as you are looking for it.
Sooner or later you will find each other!*

I read a bedtime story titled, *Are You My Mother?* to my boys. It's about a little bird that falls out of the nest before he gets to see his mother. Everyone he runs into on his new journey through life he asks, "Are you my mother?"

The little bird even tries making himself "fit in" to the lifestyles of other animals he meets just so he can have a mother, but it never seems to work.

Many of the animals make fun of the little bird, laughing at him and calling him names, but the little bird keeps on going, calling for his mother. Of course in the end the little bird calls out for his mother and his mother recognizes his voice. The two are reunited and live happily ever after.

Destiny is the "mother" in each of us. And like that little bird, we must, as if our life depended on it, cry out for "her" until we find her. Don't feel bad when you share the dreams and desires of your heart with everyone you meet and they laugh or make fun of you.

There will be many times on your journey that you will "dump" everything you know or feel on people—some you barely even know, only to have them leave, misunderstand, or not want anything to do with you. Many of them won't understand you, let alone know what to do with you or what you shared with them. But remember, you haven't made a mistake.

Even if the people you share your dreams and hopes with never help you one bit, keep sharing, and keep asking. Remember, you are looking for your mother.

Go to each person you meet or opportunity you have with the expectancy, "this could be the one." Even though it may not turn out to be "the one," keep trying! Your process of trying is eliminating everyone who is not "your mother." Don't hold back from sharing your dreams with people, because "your mother" knows your voice.

Your opportunity knows your voice. Your dream knows your voice. The people who have been appointed to help you reach your dreams know your voice. So regardless of how many people you share it with and how many times you get laughed at, made fun of, or feel rejected, sooner or later you will find "your mother."

The often-overlooked point of the story is that baby bird's mother was looking for him just as much as he was looking for her. *Be encouraged, your dream is looking for you just as hard as you are looking for it. Sooner or later you will find each other!*

8 NO ONE LOVES
A SELF-RIGHTEOUS SAVIOR

Help me to love in the midst of hate, I uttered one morning in my prayer time. Little did I know what was about to take place.

Have you ever prayed for something and then the exact opposite seems to flood every part of your life and being? All I wanted was to love people the way Jesus loved people, at least to the best of my ability.

Immediately after my noble utterance, I was greeted by some of the most hateful, arrogant, rude, obnoxious, spiteful people I had ever met in my life. It was like someone at the "main station" opened the gates and let all the *haters* out at one time.

From the person that almost ran me over with their shopping cart in the grocery store, to the one who walked toward me down the sidewalk, and with plenty of room to move over so we could both pass unharmed, stubbornly held his course for impact and crashed into my shoulder as he stormed pass me.

Did I mention he didn't apologize?

That evening I had finally settled into my office chair to finish up a little work before joining the family for a movie and ice cream. I was awakened out of my paradise moment to the sound of screeching tires. I looked out the window and saw four "hoodlums" racing down my quiet suburban street, narrowly avoiding crashing into my neighbors car, then missing my own car by inches as they slammed the car in reverse, and sped off down the street.

"You've got to be kidding me, God!" I shouted out loud as I jumped up from my desk and ran out the front door determined to bring justice at all cost. "This was my house, my neighborhood and *my land*. This is just not fair God! You have to do something about this!"

People from a party that was developing next door rushed out to see what had happened too. Suddenly, everyone was yelling and fighting over their version of what happened, and what they thought we should do next. They had obviously been drinking and were not at all concerned that they had just become more of a disruption than the car that had just sped by.

Suddenly this loud, obnoxious, rebellious, disrespectful spirit surrounded me. I had either died and gone to hell, or someone had transported me to another part of the world and I didn't know it. "I'm a prisoner in my own home," I thought to myself, "held captive by the spirit of this age and all of the filth that comes with it." GET ME OUT OF HERE LORD! I shouted under my breath.

Did I mention that I had just prayed earlier that morning for the Lord to help me "love in the midst of hate?"

For seventy-two hours after that prayer, I seemed to have lived in everything else but love. How could anyone love "people like that?" I thought to myself. Then I heard myself say to the Lord, "You loved them, didn't You, Lord? And You loved me, in all of my mess too, didn't You?"

The conviction of the Holy Spirit flooded my heart, as my eyes were opened to see what had really just happened. I hung my head and prayed, "It's not my brother, it's not my sister, it's me, oh Lord, standing in need of prayer."

"Therefore if thine enemy hunger, feed him; if he thirst, give him drink...Be not overcome of evil, but overcome evil with good." (Romans 12:20-21)

How do you love in the midst of hate?

I have discovered that when I ask God to teach me something, or to deliver me from something, I am suddenly exposed to that very thing in greater magnitude. Couldn't God just send a nice little dove to rest on my shoulder and speak sweet loving words to me? Or better yet, couldn't He prescribe a "love aid" that I could take before going to bed, and I could just wake up with a newfound love for all mankind?

Life doesn't work that way. God loves us enough to let us "work out our own salvation." If He just gets us out of what we need to work through on our own, we will remain deformed in those areas. *Can you imagine loving God but hating your neighbor?*

If we are not careful in these moments, we can become self-righteous, condescending, and curse the ones we were commanded by God to love. We begin to look down our noses at people who are not like us. People who don't live like we live, worship like we worship, believe like we believe. Suddenly, our world is just all about us. *How can we help others when all we are concerned about is ourselves?*

Do You know how to overcome self-righteousness? *You lower yourself.* Don't think more highly of yourself than you ought. Thinking more highly of ourselves than we should causes us to look down at others. It opens us up to becoming condescending and self-righteous. And *no one loves a self-righteous savior.*

Guided Prayer:

Father, forgive me today for being self-righteous. Forgive me for judging people based on my standards and life choices. Judgment is reserved for you Lord, and You alone. Help me to love like you…to simply love.

9 MY QUIRK & MY VALUE

*Your quirk doesn't disqualify you, it defines you
and sets you apart from the crowd.*

I attended a conference recently, and as I sat there watching the preachers preach and the artists share their gifts, I discovered that somewhere in the pursuit of my own destiny, I had lost something. *I had lost value in my own value.*

I knew God had called me and had given me gifts, but somewhere along the way, I lost confidence in myself and in my ability to use what He gave me. I see now that I had allowed the enemy to devalue my value. When you don't see value in yourself, your product, or your service, you won't offer it. Instead, you will keep "working on it."

Later that week, I was researching something online and clicked on a website to look at the books of a well-known speaker. Suddenly I got the thought, "those are just books, they are not really going to help you."

Not only does the enemy try to get you to devalue yourself; he will get you to devalue others. *What you devalue, you won't invest in, and more importantly, you won't receive from.*

Why would you invest in an empty gold mine? You wouldn't

Maturity helps you to see the difference between humanity and spirituality, between the gift and the one using the gift. The more mature you become, and the closer you get to people who do what you do, you begin seeing their *humanity*.

With humanity come idiosyncrasies. An idiosyncrasy is a *quirk*—a way of behaving, thinking, or feeling that is peculiar to an individual or group, especially an odd or unusual one.

If you can't get past someone's quirk, you won't receive what he or she has to offer. The danger is when you see someone's quirk as a fault. A fault, to some, disqualifies.

There is value in everything and everyone regardless of their *quirk* or what stage of the growth process they may be in. *Your quirk does not disqualify you. In fact, your quirk eventually defines you and sets you apart from the crowd.*

Avoid Becoming Critical

When we view someone's *quirk* in the wrong way, we can become critical and miss receiving from the their value.

What we are critical of in others, we are secretly critical of ourselves. Not only will we not receive from the one we are critical of, but because we are secretly critical of that very thing in ourselves, we won't use the gift God has given us to it's full capacity.

It takes a conscious effort to hold others, and yourself, in high regard. You must make a conscious decision to hold your value and self-worth in high regard. What you don't hold in high regard you won't receive from.

Becoming critical of someone because of their humanity, or

quirk, will cause you to miss the value they offer. If you are not careful, you will even discredit the value of the person along with what the person does or offers.

It's dangerous to devalue any human being, because what you are saying is that God made them worthless. If you think someone else really isn't *that great, you secretly think that about yourself and that is causing your own demise.*

As a man thinks in his heart so is he.

If you think critically of someone else, you are critical. If you are critical of others you are critical of yourself and are unknowingly sabotaging your own future.

Rediscover your own value today. Make a conscious effort to hold yourself and what you offer the world in high regard. Decide today to hold others in that same regard, even with all their quirks.

The truth is, all of us possess a quirk—a way of behaving, thinking, or feeling that makes us a little odd. Your quirk doesn't disqualify you; it makes you unique. The more unique you are, the more value you have. And the more value you have, the more benefit you have to offer others.

Guided Prayer:
Father, help me today to recognize the value in myself and in the gifts you've given me. Help me to not become critical of others or myself. Help me to embrace the way you've made me so that I can utilize my gifts to the fullest, and fulfill my destiny.

10 Deep In It

To ask someone who is fighting life's biggest battles to just think happy thoughts is like asking a soldier who is in the middle of war to just relax—it's almost impossible.

A soldier who is at war is always on guard. He is alert and ready to fight. The thought of the enemy is always looming. Scenarios of combat and ambush play like a broken record in the mind and heart of a soldier at war. **Will I make it out alive? Will I ever see my family again?** At every snap of a twig, or slam of a door, the soldier jumps to attention. His body, mind, and soul are ready to defend, to fight, or to retreat.

When that same soldier is on leave, his mind is not occupied with constant thoughts of war, but with thoughts of his family. He is thinking about catching up on baseball with his son, or reading a book to his daughter. One soft touch from his wife, and the soldier is transformed from *warrior* to *husband*; taking a walk in the moonlight with the one he loves.

I'm sure when the soldier first gets home, the first snap of a twig or slam of a door in the middle of the night invokes his involuntary warrior response. But soon after being home, he settles into some "normalcy" and he's just husband, father, son, person...*or is he?*

Is a soldier ever not a soldier? I'm not certain. Once driven by the intensity of war, many soldiers can never adjust to "normal life."

When one experiences deep dark trials or "wars" in their life, the times they are "*deep in it*" can be compared to that soldier on the battlefield. The one fighting their way through the *trials of life* is also always on guard—defending, fighting, or deciding whether or not to retreat from the hurt, pain, and agony of the "battle" they are in.

Will this battle ever end? Will I make it out alive? Will I ever fulfill my destiny?

Think Happy Thoughts

To ask someone who is fighting life's biggest battles of their lives to just *think happy thoughts* is like asking a soldier who is in the middle of war to *just relax*—it's almost impossible. The "battlefield of the mind" of the one who is fighting depression is just as real as the battlefield of war of the soldier.

To ask a soldier not to think about the enemy, or to not worry if every bump his Humvee passes over is a bomb, would be foolish. Why? Because he's at war, and that's the way a soldier thinks when he is at war. In fact, he is probably still alive because he thinks that way.

Similarly, asking a person who is deep in depression, failure, doubt, or fear to just "snap out of it," "just think about something else," "deal with it," or better yet, "just get over it," is like asking that solider to think happy thoughts during times of war.

Every season of war and of life requires certain attitudes, behaviors, thought processes, and emotions designed to get one through that season. There is victory in learning to be okay with where you are at, knowing that soon you will receive your orders to go home—a furlough, a time to recover, a time of no enemy, no concern, nothing to fear, and no need to hide.

That's the place one needs to find between "tours of duty," both in the battlefield of war and the battlefield of everyday life.

Wherever You Are, Be There

Are you in the battlefield of war for real? *Be there*! You are equipped to be where you are. Stand your ground, defend, fight, and even on occasions, if the need arises, retreat.

Wherever you are, be there. Your orders have been processed; your furlough is coming. And when it comes and it's time to return home, be there!

Are you fighting a war of a different kind? Do you find yourself in the battlefield of life? Depression, fear, jobless, homeless, or hopeless? *Be there!*

You are equipped to be where you are! Stand your ground, defend, fight, and even on occasions, retreat. But where you are, be there! Remain confident. Your orders have been processed; your furlough is coming. Your relief has been summoned.

In a moment, in the twinkling of an eye, relief will arrive. Joy and hope will soon return. Soon life will be good again. Look up...look up, your redemption draweth nigh.

Remember: Where you are is not who you are!

Guided Prayer:

Father, give me strength to be where I am. Not just to exist, but to be effective, to make a difference, to defend, to protect and to defeat the enemies that come against me. Thank you that you have equipped me for war and for peace; to succeed both on the battlefield of war, and in the battlefield of my mind.

11 Don't Let Your Next Opportunity Find You In Rollers

The greatest tragedy is for the opportunity that you've prayed for to pass you by because you were left unrecognizable by the last tragic cycle you went through.

*P*ain causes us to withdraw. Great pain has a tendency to force us to retreat. Difficulty causes us to withdraw rather than ready ourselves for the next opportunity.

Sometimes the pain of what we are going through damages our self-image so much that we lose all consideration of how we look. Seeing ourselves in the mirror at our *worst*, we conclude, "Who would want anything to do with someone like me?"

There is a passage of scripture in Isaiah 30:22 that says, "Thou shall cast them away as a menstruous cloth; thou shalt say unto it, 'Get thee hence.'"

Now don't tune me out too quickly. I'm not a woman, and don't claim to know what a woman goes through during her time of cycle. But I bet I could get a few men to agree with me, (and even some honest women), that a woman can be sometimes less than desirable to be around during her *cycle*.

Some women even suffer great pain with their menstrual cycle. Some can become very emotional at the drop of a hat and some are even bed bound with the pain of their "moment."

Can you liken that to someone who is in the midst of the

"bloodiness," most "painful," "yuck" of "life's cycle?"

Come on, stay with me! Divorce, bankruptcy, the unexpected tragic death of a child, foreclosure of your first home, the loss of a job you've had for twenty years, failure of the dream that you've been dreaming of all your life.

Can you relate to the hurt, the mood swings, the anger, and the pain that someone feels when he or she is going through his or her "cycle" of life?

It's an interesting fact that a woman's cycle, even in all that pain, is designed by the Great Designer to purge, to cleanse, and to prepare a woman's body for something new.

Medical journals tell us that having regular menstrual cycles is a sign that important parts of a woman's body are working. The menstrual cycle provides important body chemicals, called hormones, to keep the woman healthy. The menstrual cycle also prepares the woman's body for pregnancy each month.

Preparation for pregnancy doesn't guarantee pregnancy.

If you've been *purged* and *prepared*, but you don't re-engage in intimacy—one of the hardest things to do after you've been hurt so bad—you will remain purged and prepared, but you will not become pregnant. You will pass through cycle after cycle until you decide it's time to get dressed up again!

Sooner or later you have to decide that it's time to *do your hair, paint your nails*, and get back to *presenting yourself* to the next opportunity, so that it does not pass you by.

The greatest tragedy is for the opportunity that you've prayed to pass you by because you were left unrecognizable by the last tragic cycle you went through. Opportunity knocks, only to find you standing on the threshold with your *hair in rollers*, your teeth not brushed, and in your fuzzy slippers and jammies that haven't been washed for a week.

A menstrual cycle indicates that important parts of you are working properly, and that your body is being prepared for pregnancy! I submit to you friend, that *the cycle of life you may find yourself in is not meant to destroy you, but to purge you and prepare you for what's ahead.*

Let go of what has happened to you! Stop crying over who didn't help you, or who left you. We've all got stories. Make something of yours! Tell your story after you've used it to catapult you into your promise.

What you are going through is preparing you to become pregnant with an even bigger promise. *Loss and pain are always a part of something bigger in you.* The cycle of pain purges us and prepares us for new life. You can't get pregnant without going through a cycle. But don't cheat yourself out of the benefit of your cycle—pregnancy with new life.

Have you lost your job? Get up, take a shower, get dressed, and be ready for the opportunity of employment that is about to knock on your door. Did he leave you with the kids and the bills and the broken down car? Throw that menstrual cloth away! Say to it, "Get thee behind me!"

Dress your self up woman of God! Take your life back man of God! *Don't allow what you've been through to be in vain.* Don't answer the door of opportunity in rollers. Get ready for your new opportunity; it's knocking at your door!

Guided Prayer:

Father, help me today to get back up, and get back in the game of life! Help me to throw off this "menstruous cloth." Help me to draw strength from my cycles of defeat and failure that I've been through, and give me today, Lord, a new perspective of myself and the opportunity that's before me. Help me to see me as you see me!

Today is my day! I say, "enough is enough." I choose today to get my self ready for the next opportunity that is before me. I will no longer lay by the wayside of life feeling sorry for myself! What's done is done. I choose today to use everything that's happened to me to catapult me into my destiny.

No more rollers! Today is my day!

12 MATURITY & IMMATURITY

Perfection and imperfection, completeness and incompleteness, can't coexist. One gives way to the other.

*W*hen the complete and perfect comes, the incomplete and imperfect will vanish away (become antiquated, void, and superseded). 1 Corinthians 13:10.

As we strive to be all God has created us to be, we pass through many stages of growth. A major concern of the one pursuing perfection is, "Will I ever get there?"

Some say you never arrive. But if life, and your calling, require you to arrive, and you never do, how will you ever be who you know you were created to be?

One whose life purpose is to fulfill their life's purpose continually searches the deep parts of their heart and soul questioning what needs to stay and what needs to go.

The Apostle Paul encourages us in 1 Corinthians 13 that when the complete and perfect (total) comes, the incomplete and imperfect will vanish away (become antiquated, void, and superseded).

It's exciting to know that *perfection or completeness has its timing.* Paul says, *when* the complete and perfect comes, not *if.*

It's also worth noting that perfection and imperfection,

completeness and incompleteness, can't coexist; one gives way to the other. The scripture tells us that it's the incomplete and imperfect that will vanish away.

Friend, I encourage you today that the path you are on is leading you somewhere. Your destiny is before you and your steps have been ordered; no matter how difficult they may seem right now. And in your rising up and falling down, succeeding and failing, your complete, perfect (total) is coming, and *your incomplete and imperfect is vanishing away.*

Don't fight the process, just go with the flow; it's taking you somewhere.

13 MONSTERS IN THE CLOSET

On the other side of your greatest opportunity
lies your greatest opposition.

F or a great door and effectual is opened unto me, and there are many adversaries. (1 Corinthians 16:9)

A door is access, opportunity, an opening, or a way in to or out of something. Paul describes this door as not just as any door, but a *great door.*

This was not just any opportunity, or another opportunity, but THE opportunity. Paul was so sure that this door was THE door he had been waiting on that he changed his plans so he could remain in Ephesus until this door was fully opened.

(It would behoove many reading this to change your plans to wait for the door in front of you to fully open before making your decision to go elsewhere.)

Paul goes on to describe this door as *effectual.* Effectual means: *producing or able to produce a desired effect or result.* The door, or opportunity, that was opened before Paul was not just a door, not even just a great door, but an effectual door. It was *one with the means, or power, to produce a desired affect.*

This great door of opportunity that was opening before Paul possessed the power to bring about the desired results of his heart. (*Handle the door, or opportunity, that is opened, or opening, before you very wisely.*)

Effectual Opportunity

You need to know that this opportunity is not just another opportunity. This opportunity is not just going to get you from one season to the next. It's not just going to just hold you over until something else better comes along. This opportunity is the *effectual opportunity.*

The door that is open before you has the power to produce or make manifest your life's dream. Your Destiny awaits you on the other side of this great and effectual door.

Many Adversaries

Paul goes on to teach us in 1 Corinthians 16:9 that, "For a great door and effectual is opened unto me, and there are *many adversaries.*" Remember, on the other side of your door are many adversaries—*monsters in the closet.*

Webster defines an adversary as: *one that contends with, opposes, or resists: an enemy.*

On the other side of your greatest opportunity lies your greatest opposition. On the other side of access is denial. On the other side of momentum is resistance—one door, many adversaries.

On the Other Side

Know this: On the other side of your great and effectual door are multiple opposing forces with one goal in mind—**resist you!**

To resist means: to exert oneself so as to counteract or defeat or to withstand the force or effect of. *Resistance is always on the other side of opportunity.*

Resistance is not an inward pull; it is an outward push. Resistance is not an inward force pulling you back; it is an outward force pushing against your attempt to go forward.

As you walk through your great and effectual door, it may appear futile at times. However, remember that our faith is not in the open door, but in knowing that the One who opened the door for us is greater than the one standing in the doorway opposing us.

Your Adversary

Be certain you know who your adversary is. 1 Peter 5:8 says, "Be sober, be vigilant; because your adversary the devil, as a roaring lion, walketh about, seeking whom he may devour."

The Bible is clear that our adversary is the devil. How do you defeat your adversary? YOU RESIST HIM IN FAITH! 1 Peter 5:9 says, "Whom *resist steadfast in the faith.*" WOW! You resist that which resists you.

In order to win, someone's resistance has to be stronger than the others. If that which resists you is stronger than the resistance in you, it will win. But if that which is in you is stronger than the force that resists you, you will win.

Not only do you have to resist the adversary, you have to resist him *in faith.* In other words, *you have to believe that your resistance of the adversary is stronger than his resistance of you.*

Be of Good Cheer

If you're wondering whether or not you are strong enough to win, I have good news for you. John 16:33 says, "In the world ye shall have tribulation: but be of good cheer; I have overcome the world."

You can be sure that there is an undeniable adversary working against you, and that adversary would love nothing more than to see you never step foot across the threshold of your effectual great door. 1 John 4:4 says, "Ye are of God, little children, and have overcome them: because greater is He that is in you than he that is in the world."

Be encouraged by the fact that *the One who has created you has already defeated the one who opposes you.*

Guided Prayer:

Father, thank you for the great door of opportunity that you have set before me. I pray for your strength to overcome the adversary and the courage to conquer that which contends against me, that I may be successful at what I do and where I go today. In Jesus' name, amen.

14 WHAT ARE YOU WAITING ON?

*Help, at the wrong time, can actually leave one
undeveloped and as a result, inept for life.*

What if the "breakthrough" you are waiting on is in you? What if what you need is already in you? And what if the very situation you face is really an answer to your prayer? Would you welcome it or rebuke it?

It's an odd realization that the pain of what you are going through is the very thing that is making you. In essence, it is the answer to your prayer. And when you come through what you are going through, you will be both who, and where, you want to be.

Life sends you the very situation or person that "grinds" on you the most, that one who pushes all your buttons. Because sometimes, the very thing you want to be delivered from must come against you to actually deliver you. First, to flush out or reveal that it's in you to begin with, and secondly to help you develop the strength you need to actually defeat it.

The "thing" that's coming against you is really in you. Because if what comes against you from the outside is not inside you in some form, what comes against you from the outside wouldn't bother you.

It's like injecting someone with a virus so that their body goes to work and develops the antibody that saves their life.

Isn't that amazing? Inject you with something that you want so desperately to be free from?

Why can't God just take out of us this "thing" we want to be free from? After all, He's God, He can do anything, right? He doesn't just take it out, because if He did we would never develop the strength it takes to remain free.

True, lasting freedom only comes through metamorphosis— the process of being reborn or born again into something new.

A caterpillar who is helped out of his cocoon will never develop into the butterfly. Why? Because *help, at the wrong time, can actually leave one undeveloped and as a result, inept for life.*

You are not who you've never developed to be. If you "get there" on the outside before you "get there" on the inside, you will fall short of your destiny.

If I would have known, to begin with, that self-development was so hard, I'm not sure I would have signed up for the trip. But at a certain point, self-development becomes addictive.

You know that what you are about to go through is going to hurt like hell, but you almost welcome it, even at times urge it on, as if to say, "Come on, give me your best shot." Because you know the growth—the personal growth—you will experience by going through.

You almost develops an "attitude of gratitude" for the atrocities, challenges, tragedies, and difficulties life brings your way, because you finally realize it's all making you into who you were created to be

Welcome what will make you. Rebuke what will destroy you. But before you do either, make sure you know the difference.

15 WHERE DOES GOD FIND HIS NEXT AMERICAN IDOL?

*God chooses the foolish, the weak, and the base things
of the world to put to shame things that are mighty.*

God chooses the *foolish things* of the world to put to shame the wise, and God has chosen the *weak things* of the world to put to shame the things which are mighty; and the *base things* of the world and the things which are despised God has chosen, and the things which are not, to bring to nothing the things that are, that no flesh should glory in His presence. (1 Corinthians 1:27)

The Bible tells us that God chooses the *foolish*, the *weak*, and the *base* things of the world to put to shame things that are mighty.

Foolish: Lacking in sense, judgment, or discretion, trifling or insignificant.

Weak: Lacking in physical strength. Lacking in moral strength or courage. (Frail, imperfect, weak). Deficient or lacking in some skill.

Base: Not adhering to ethical or moral principles. Of low birth (lowly status, illegitimate).

The message in 1 Corinthians is pretty clear—***God doesn't do things like the world.***

Popularity

Friend, if you are waiting to become "popular" to finally be successful, what if it never happens? If you're waiting to reach the billboard charts to reveal your greatness, what if you never make it? *What if you are one the world never approves of you or selects you as their next American Idol?* Take comfort, friend, God has a different selection process than the world.

The world says you have to be great to be noticed. The world says you have to be the first, the best, the notable, in order to really be someone. The world says you have to have a superstar voice, look, product, or personality if you are ever going to make it.

If your feeling like you will never get a break, like no one could ever possibly notice you, remember, God chooses *the foolish*—the things that don't make sense to the natural mind. He uses *the weak*—the deficient and lacking. And God uses *the base*—the lowly, and those who appear lost and of no value whatsoever, to do great and mighty things!

God uses the foolish things to put to shame the wise. He chooses the weak things to put to shame things that are mighty. God chooses the base things—the seemingly insignificant and the despised—to bring to nothing the things that are. **God chooses things that are not to bring to nothing the things that are.**

So, if you are feeling like you are one of those *foolish, weak,* or *base,* or one who isn't anything or anybody, hold your head up high, square you shoulders and get ready for God to use you mightily!

Why would God use someone seemingly insignificant? Why would God choose to use someone who has never accomplished anything great in their life, or who is not on the cover of Vogue, Vanity Fair, or Time?

Why would God use someone who doesn't even have a YouTube Video or a website? Because when you make it to the top, God wants you to give all of the credit to Him.

Google Didn't Make You...God did!

Friend, may I be bold with you? *Google didn't make you, God did!* Your job didn't make you wealthy, God did! You didn't get your good looks from your Momma, God gave them to you!

God gave you everything you have!

The breath in your lungs to sing your top billboard songs, the sanity you have to manage that business. Everything, everything, everything we have comes from God!

If it's been a while since you've said "thanks," would you take a minute today to thank God for what He has given you and done in your life? *Give God the glory for who you are, not Google.*

16 LET ZEALOUS INDIGNATION ARISE!

Hear ye the word of the Lord—Isaiah 42

I have for a long time held My peace, I have been still and restrained Myself. Now I will cry out like a woman in travail, I will gasp and pant together. I will march out like a champion, like a warrior. I will stir up my zeal. With a shout, I will raise the battle cry and triumph over My enemies. I will now lay waste the mountains and hills and dry up all their vegetation; I will turn the rivers into islands, and I will dry up the pools.

I will bring the blind by a way that they know not; I will lead them in paths that they have not known. I will make darkness into light before them and make uneven places into a plain. These things I have determined to do for them, and I will not leave them forsaken.

Turn back those who trust in graven images! Utterly put to shame those who say to molten images, You are our gods. Hear, you deaf! And look, you blind, that you may see!

For too long we've sat silently by watching injustice, immorality, and hypocrisy rule and dictate. We've slept with tolerance in the name of grace. We bore illegitimate, ignorant, weak and worldly off spring, having the form of Godliness but lacking the power thereof!

CHOOSE this day whom you shall serve! If the world is your god, them serve it! Stop living behind bumper stickers and jargon that isn't yours—your language gives you away.

The Lord says, "I would rather you be hot or cold, but if you remain lukewarm I will spew you out of my mouth." Tolerance has become your god!

Arise Men and Women! Arise Sons and Daughters! Take up your sword. Arm yourself!

They are a people robbed and plundered; they are all snared in holes and hidden in houses of bondage. They have become a prey, with no one to deliver them. They are a spoil, with no one to say, "Restore them!"

Who is there among you who will give ear to this?

Who will listen and hear in the time to come. *Who will ARISE? Who will SEPARATE? Who will GO? Who will DO? Who will STAND UP and be counted?*

17 Don't Settle For Sour

*Go ahead! Dance and shout over your victory
again. Break free from that sadness! The day of
your captivity is over once and for all!*

When we face difficulty for extended periods of time, we can develop the habit of being sour or sad. Let's face it, when you can't feel glad the next best thing is to feel sad. At least you are feeling something.

The danger is we can develop a habit, and in extreme cases, even a satisfaction in feeling sour and sad. When victory begins to break through in our lives we can have a tendency to hold back being glad.

We must be able to let go of our attraction to "sad" and give ourselves permission to be glad.

Have you ever heard bad news for so long that when you get good news you are really happy down deep inside but don't want to show it, because, after all, what if the good news doesn't last? What if this happy feeling I have doesn't stay? What if the victory I feel starting to break loose in my soul never manifests, never comes to fruition? What then?

I'm writing to people who have hurt for so long, you don't know what it's like not to hurt. In fact you are so afraid to be glad because every other time you've been glad for a moment, something in your life goes wrong again. The wind of defeat blows you over, and you find yourself sad all over.

Sad will sometimes try to convince you that he is your new identity, your "new norm." To break totally free, you must trust that the glad you are starting to feel again will last this time.

Your joy, peace, happiness, fulfillment, and contentment are returning to you. You are being restored. God has turned your captivity and is restoring your baskets. Your time of affliction is over. You have moved from crucifixion to resurrection. For your shame you are receiving double.

Get your praise back on! Pick up your tambourine! Don't allow the enemy to steal your victory! Trust that the glad you feel is real. It will work this time! Stop faking you are sad when you are really glad!

Break the cycle of sadness by embracing gladness. And if others around you don't understand you, just ask them politely to get out the way! Tell them, "It's been a long time coming, and I am glad again."

Go ahead! Dance and shout over your victory again. Break free from that sadness! *The day of your captivity is over once and for all!*

18 DON'T BE TOO QUICK TO BUILD A TABERNACLE

What we do with what was meant to be a "moment of a lifetime" and never intended to be "for a lifetime," could cause us to miss our true destiny.

Jesus took Peter, James and John his brother, to the mountain where he was transfigured before them. Suddenly Moses and Elijah appeared talking with them. (Matthew 17:4)

Can you imagine what that would have been like?

Peter said, "Jesus, Lord, it is good for us to be here: let us make here three tabernacles; one for you, one for Moses and one for Elijah." Suddenly the voice of God echoes from the heavens, "This is my beloved Son, in whom I'm well pleased; hear ye him."

At the booming voice of God, the disciples hit the ground and were afraid. Jesus came and touched them. He said, "Arise, and be not afraid." When the disciples opened their eyes, there was no one there but Jesus. Jesus gathered his disciples and headed back down the mountain.

Don't be too quick to build a tabernacle around every "mountain top moment" you have in life.

One definition for tabernacle is "a dwelling place." Too often we have this wonderful encounter with the Lord and we get this awesome revelation or thought, or have this "one of a kind" experience, and we instantly begin trying to think how to build a "tabernacle" around it—a *dwelling place*.

We try "putting up walls"—make plans to sell the house, pick the wedding date, or form a committee to choose the right color carpet—around something that was simply "a moment."

In this passage of scripture, Peter said, "It is good for us to be here." Every *good place* is not intended to be a *dwelling place*.

What if the guy you had dinner with—you know, the one who brought you flowers, opened your car door, and made you feel so beautiful and special inside—is not "Mr. Right." He's not "the one" you are to marry or *build a tabernacle around*, but someone God simply brought your way, for *a moment*, to remind you of how beautiful and special you really are?

> "Sometimes what happens to you is simply a moment; something God wants you to experience, and then move on."

What if that name that came to you in the midnight hour—you know, the one that has you up at nights, pacing the floor, praying for hours—is not the name of a church, ministry, or business you are supposed to build, but simply a revelation of the next season God is bringing you into?

What if we built a tabernacle—a permanent dwelling place—around something that was never intended to be permanent?

I've learned, after following the purpose of God for more than thirty years, that every experience we have is not a "sign" of something we should be doing. Sometimes what happens to us is simply a moment; something God wants you and I to experience, and then move on.

Did you notice in the passage that as quickly as this *mountain top moment* the disciples experienced came, it left?

Can you imagine building a permanent dwelling place around a temporary experience?

What we do with what was meant to be a "moment of a lifetime" and never intended to be "for a lifetime," could cause us to miss our true destiny. The disciples wanted to *dwell in* what Jesus just wanted them to *experience*.

The next time you have a mountain top moment, an epiphany, or revelation, be sure to wait it out before you start ordering supplies and drawing up the blueprints for your "tabernacle." It may be just a *moment* and not a permanent *dwelling place*.

19 PERFECTION

*When it feels like you are the only one left on the
planet who knows how to do it "right," resist
the urge to see things "wrong" in others.*

*I*mperfection is magnified in the presence of perfection.
The closer we come to perfection, or maturity, the more
the immaturity, or "imperfection" of others is magnified to us.

"I wouldn't have done it that way."

"Why don't they just...!"

The "wrong" in others is magnified when the "right" in us
begins to shine. The truth is, what we think is "wrong" in
others, is not wrong at all; it's just where they are right now.

If we are honest, where they are is where we just came from
ourselves. But when we're in the midst of "it," we can't see "it."
When you come out of "it," everything becomes more clear.

It is critical for us, at this moment of "going to the next level"
or "coming into our own," that we guard against becoming
critical, puffed up and prideful. *The moment of coming into
one's own is when our flesh is the most susceptible to an attack.*

Pride is perverted authority. God has created us to be *proud*
of who we are. God has created us to "rule and reign," but

pride—*the elevation of one's self over another for the purpose of simply being superior*, is perverted authority, and is the enemy's breeding ground for destruction. That kind of pride comes before a fall.

At this moment, when you feel the real you begin to rise up inside, when you feel yourself passing from one level to another, it can seem like suddenly everyone is against you, or like no one you meet can do anything right.

When it feels like you are the only one left on the planet who knows how to do it "right," resist the urge to see things "wrong" in others. Remain thankful that the Lord has brought you to a new level, into a *new land*. Remember that just a moment ago that was you.

Self Righteous

Guard yourself from becoming critical or *self-righteous*. Embrace your promotion, but remember that if it weren't for God, you would still be going around that same mountain again and again.

"Self" righteousness sees its "self" as right and everyone else as wrong. But remember, there is not one good, no not one!

Your "self" is no better than anyone else's "self." We are all flesh and blood. Every human being, regardless of race, gender, color or creed, deserves the same universal respect. Remember that the highest form of righteousness is not defined by self or flesh, but by right standing with God.

As *flesh and blood* I am no better than any other "self" on this planet. But having accepted Christ as my Savior, it is no longer I, "self," who lives, but "Christ"—the complete work of God—that lives in me. The life I now live in the flesh, "self," I live by the faith in the Son of God who loved me and gave Him "self" for me. (Galatians 2:20) I have laid down my "self" so I can pick up His! Oh, praise God!

Governing Your Self

You have the right to govern your "self," but the real you, your spirit, is under the headship and authority of Jesus Christ— God in the flesh.

He has total control over you, because He has purchased you with the greatest price known to mankind—*blood*.

Jesus Christ gave His life that you might have life, not "self," and have it more abundantly.

You have the right to govern your "self" but Christ, who is the propitiation of sin, and who has paved The Way to eternal righteousness for all mankind, governs your spirit. You just have to receive it.

The End

The world *was*, the world *is*, and the world *will be*...then *the end* will come.

You are absolutely in charge of your "self." You have the right to choose to live any way you want to. You can choose any lifestyle you want and stake your claim that you are forever remaining "true to who you are."

But remember that your "self" will come to an end. And when that happens, your spirit will continue to be for all eternity. *It*

is only when you come to the end of who you think you are that
you will come to know who you really are.

"But for now we see in a mirror dimly; but then face to face:
now I know in part; but then shall I know even as also I am
known." (1 Corinthians 13:12)

Eternal Separation

There will come a day when you will know yourself as you are
known. That will be the moment of truth. If at this point you
have never given the governing of your spirit—the real you—
over to the Lordship of Jesus Christ, you will be *separated*.

The goats—those who have chosen to govern themselves—
will be gathered to one side, and the sheep—those who have
given themselves to the governing of Christ Jesus—the other.

On that great and notable Day of Judgment, the King of
Kings and Lord of Lords will stand at the Judgment seat, and
spirit after spirit (one light of man after another) will come and
stand before God Almighty to bare record of the decisions they
have made with the "self" and the "life" they have been given.

For those who have accepted *The Way*, *The Truth*, and *The
Life*, the Eternal Judge will bare record of your name recorded
in The Lamb's book of life, and instruct you to "enter ye in thou
good and faithful servant."

But if you have never surrendered your life to the governing
of The One who created you, if you have chosen to govern
your "self," and refused the life of Christ, you will stand before
Almighty God—Eternal Judge—and have to justify your "self"
before Him. And we are all but as *filthy rags*.

Who dares declare their own selves good in the sight of Almighty God?

To govern your "self," friend, means you accept the *eternal responsibility* and consequences for your *self* and *spirit*.

All have sinned and fallen short of the glory of God. No man is good, no not one. And the wages of sin is death.

Nature Reveals The Truth

Look into nature. It's apparent that there is more to life than what we know. God, the Eternal Supreme Creator, is seen in every part of our world, so much so that *all man will be without excuse*.

The Spirit of the Lord is in the earth beckoning His sons and daughters to surrender their lives to Him. Time is of the essence. The Way has been made. The Way Maker is waiting. To accept Eternal Life is to live; to deny it is death. *Choose ye this day whom you shall serve.*

I challenge you today, friend. If this world is your god, then serve it. But if God is your God, then serve Him! Sell out! Make God your passion, your consumption, your conviction, and your every waking moment. *Ask, seek*, and *knock*, while there is time.

For there will come a day when every knee shall bow and every tongue shall confess that Jesus is Lord...*regardless of what we have decided.*

20 THRIVE, DON'T STRIVE

The place of rest is truly the only place you
can be the person have been designed to be.

O ne of the last hurdles you will overcome on your journey to destiny is learning to *thrive*, and not *strive*.

The scriptures tell us that weeping may endure for a night season, but joy cometh in the morning.

There is a season for weeping, for struggle, for fighting, and for striving to get ahead. But you were never designed to always strive for what you want in life, you were designed to thrive in what has already been provided for you.

To strive is to quarrel, to contend, or to fight for. Some people are not content unless they are fighting for something. Some find their very self-worth and identity in the struggle.

You were not designed to strive forever; you were designed to thrive.

The book of Genesis in the Bible tells us that on the seventh day God *rested*. All that God had planned to do was finished. He never has to go back to work again. Jesus Christ said the same thing on Calvary when He declared, "it is finished."

Everything God had to do was done; therefore, He rested. Everything Jesus had to do before He was to go to the cross was done, therefore, He said, "It is finished."

The works of God are finished for eternity, and friend, you and I are a part of His finished work. We are His workmanship, created in Christ Jesus. *Therefore we can rest from our works too.*

Hebrews 4:10 declares, "For he who has entered into his rest, has also hath ceased from his own works." Finished work doesn't require effort. So many Christians are "doing the right thing," but for all the wrong reasons.

We're praying, reading our Bible, going to Church, quoting our scriptures, thinking positively, loving our spouse, playing with our kids, but we are doing it *anxiously.*

We are striving, working to arrive at a place that access has already been made available to us…for free!

Rest doesn't require effort, except the effort it takes to rest. For some, even resting is an effort.

Today, be aware of your own *angst.* Be aware of the tightness in your chest, your "hurry-up-so-we-can-have-fun" attitude. Today choose to enter into rest—the place of fulfillment, accomplishment, and completion. After all, Jesus gave His life for it. Accept it and enter into it.

Rest is truly the only place you can be the person have been designed to be. **Today, don't strive; THRIVE!**

21 The Missing Link

*Even the smallest of accomplishments can
fuel the greatest of achievements.*

While I was watching the 2008 Summer Olympics, I discovered something that the Olympians had in their lives that was missing in the lives of many people—a gold medal. Not necessarily the medal itself, but what the medal represented.

Many have dreamed about it, desired it, and even started working toward it, but most have fallen short of it.

Watching Phelps swim for nine gold medals, Patterson taking the gold in women's gymnastics, and all of the other athletes achieving their dreams, made me realize that the missing link in many people's lives is *accomplishment*. It's the finish line, the win, the "I did it!"

The words "good try" or "you gave it your best shot," are only *silver* and *bronze* medals for the Olympian whose heart is set on gold. The only spot for him or her is on the center of the podium.

Year after year they train for a shot at becoming the best in the world, the pinnacle of accomplishment and self-satisfaction. The moment they cross the finish line, clear the bar, or stick the dismount, the champion within screams, "I knew I could do it!"

The power of accomplishment is limitless in its ability to create and achieve. The power of accomplishment harnessed can save a life, build a city, or even change a nation. Accomplishment can turn hopelessness into hope, losers into winners, failure into success, and tragedy into triumph. Even the smallest of accomplishments can fuel the greatest of achievements.

Have you ever started something but never finished it, then beat yourself up for not finishing it? The most miserable life is a life filled with undone. Many people's lives are filled with half-finished dreams, plans, ideas, and intentions. They have settled for "good try" and "you gave it your best shot," while all along they truly desire the "I did it!"

Achievement:

Webster defines achievement as the act of accomplishing or finishing something by means of exertion, skill, practice and perseverance.

Achievement always seems easy in the "dream" stage. It's when the exertion, skill, practice, and perseverance are required that most fall short. I wonder how many people go through life never reaching their "gold."

Day after day, as a Hospice Chaplain, I met people who had come to the end of their race in life. Some had their gold—their family, their peace of eternal salvation, their memory of making a difference in world they lived in—but so many others were left with the *pain of regret*. They had been busy running the race, but never attaining the prize.

As people approach the final moments of their lives here on this earth, you can see in their eyes that they would give anything to have one more opportunity to "cross the finish line," "clear the bar," or "stick the dismount," and to hear the champion within say, "I knew I could do it!"

Finishing the Unfinished

What about you? What have you left undone in your life that you still have time to accomplish? Maybe it is competing in the Olympics. Maybe it's finishing that book you started writing all those years ago. Or maybe it's completing your education. Maybe it's simply sending a card you've been meaning to send to that someone special.

> "To hold 'the gold' is the power to change one's life forever."

Whether it's an unfinished dream, an unfinished New Year's resolution or an unfinished promise, *finishing the unfinished is the missing link.* To hold the gold is the power to change one's life forever.

About the Author

Jeff Crume

I was called to preach at the early age of seventeen. During a revival service I was attending, the preacher called me out of the audience, put his hand on my head, and spoke **Isaiah 61** over me—*The Spirit of the Lord is upon me for He has anointed me to preach.*

Isaiah 61 was the same scripture that the Lord gave my mom for me when I was born, and has been the guiding force of my life for the past thirty-plus years. ***One word can change someone's life; it did mine.***

My heart's passion and life's mission is to see people come to the saving knowledge of Jesus Christ, and to find and fulfill their divine destiny. I know that even my "speech" about God may turn some people away, but I have come to realize that God's opinion of me matters more to me than man's.

I live to reflect, not to attract. I live to reveal, not to retain. I point the way; I am not the way. If my life helps someone else see The Way, I am complete.

— Jeff Crume

for more information visit:
www.jeffcrumeministries.org

MY MOMENTS

A life worth living is a life worth recording.
(Use the following pages to record your destiny moments)

_____

_____

_____

_____

_____

_____

_____

_____

_____

DESTINY MOMENTS

_____

_____

_____

_____

_____

_____

_____

_____

_____

_____

_____

_____

_____

_____

_____

_____

_____

_____

_____

_____

_____

_____

_____

_____

_____

DESTINY MOMENTS

_____

_____

_____

_____

_____

_____

_____

_____

_____

_____

_____

www.ingramcontent.com/pod-product-compliance
Lightning Source LLC
Chambersburg PA
CBHW071102040426
42443CB00013B/3374